Cover *Members of the Iranian Islamic Revolutionary Guard who have been responsible for many attacks on shipping in the Gulf.*

Frontispiece *The Singapore-flagged tanker* Norman Atlantic *starts to sink after it was hit by an Iranian gunboat in the Strait of Hormuz.*

THE
GULF WAR

Nick Childs

Wayland

The Arab-Israeli Issue
The Conflict in Afghanistan
The Division of Berlin
The Crisis in Central America
The Cuban Missile Crisis
The Falklands Conflict
The Gulf War
The Hungarian Uprising

The Partition of India
The Irish Question
The Revolution in Iran
The Korean War
The Rise of Solidarity
The Crisis in South Afri
The Suez Crisis
The Vietnam War

Author: Nick Childs, a senior current affairs talks writer and political
commentator, BBC Arabic Service.

Editor: Clare Chandler

First published in 1988 by
Wayland (Publishers) Ltd
61 Western Road, Hove
East Sussex BN3 1JD, England

British Library Cataloguing Publication Data

Childs, Nick
  The Gulf War.
  1. Iran. Wars with Iraq, 1980–
  I. Title
  955'.054

  ISBN 1-85210-526-7

Printed and bound in Great Britain at The Bath Press, Avon

Contents

1
Iraq Invades

Iraqi Military Communique No 1 (1329 GMT, 22 September 1980): AT 1200 TODAY, 22 SEPTEMBER, OUR AIR FORCE RAIDED MILITARY BASES AND AIRPORTS DEEP INSIDE IRANIAN TERRITORY, INFLICTING HEAVY LOSSES.....

Communique No 2 (1812 GMT, 22 September): OUR AIR FORMATIONS CONTINUED BETWEEN 1500–1800 HOURS TO CARRY OUT THEIR COMBAT DUTIES BY ATTACKING IRANIAN MILITARY TARGETS INFLICTING HEAVY DAMAGE.....

Communique No 3 (0600 GMT, 23 September): AT 0300 TODAY, 23 SEPTEMBER, OUR LAND FORCES ADVANCED TOWARDS THE DESIGNATED TARGETS..... INSIDE IRAN IN ORDER TO SUPPRESS THE RACIST GOVERNMENT IN IRAN, TO DEFLATE ITS CONCEIT, AND TO FORCE IT TO SUBMIT TO THE NEW FAIT ACCOMPLI AND TO RESPECT IRAQI SOVEREIGNTY.....

One of the main objectives of Iraq's invasion was to capture the great Iranian port of Khorramshahr. Here, an Iraqi soldier, part of the force laying siege to Khorramshahr, pumps machine-gun fire into the city.

On 22 September 1980, waves of Iraqi MiG fighters streaked into Iran to attack ten military bases and airports across the country, including a military air base just outside the Iranian capital, Tehran. These missions were clearly meant to destroy the bulk of the Iranian air force on the ground. In fact, they failed. But, even so, fifteen hours after the first air raids had begun, Iraqi ground forces started moving into Iranian territory along a 550 km front.

The main Iraqi thrust was across the Shatt al-Arab waterway, the disputed southern boundary between the two countries. From there, the Iraqis pushed on into the Iranian border province of Khuzestan, with its vast oil wealth and large population of ethnic Arabs.

Initially, the invasion went well. Iran was still in a state of

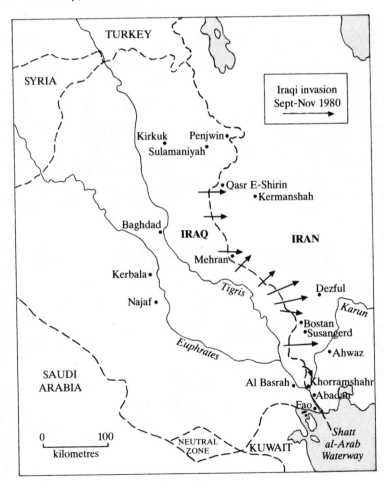

Right *The Iraqis invaded Iran along a 550 km front. But the main thrust was across the Shatt-al-Arab waterway in the south.*

10

some chaos, not much more than a year and a half after
revolution had swept the Shah from power, and Ayatollah
Ruhollah Khomeini had taken over at the head of a new
Islamic republic.

The Iranians quickly retaliated against Iraq with air raids on the Iraqi capital, Baghdad, and other cities and towns. But, on the ground, the Iranian army was almost nowhere to be seen. Instead, the main opposition to the Iraqis came from the new republic's lightly-armed revolutionary militia,

the Pasdaran. And, over the flat, dusty, open country of Khuzestan, they were no match for the Iraqi armour and infantry.

But the story was very different in the towns. There, the Iranian resistance was much tougher. In the first days of

Iran's Abadan refinery was a prime target of the Iraqi air force, and its destruction has seriously damaged Iran's oil exports.

their invasion, the Iraqis captured only Qasr E-Shirin, in the north, and Mehran, right on the border in the central sector of the war front.

In Khuzestan, the Iraqi advance was halted in front of Dezful, with its important military bases and oil installations, and the provincial capital of Ahwaz. On the east bank of the Shatt, the Iraqis announced the capture of the great port of Khorramshahr four times before it actually fell on 26 October, after four weeks of siege and shattering artillery bombardment. Even then, the Iraqis never had full control of Khorramshahr. And Abadan never fell, even though its huge oil refinery was devastated in the opening stages of the conflict, sending great columns of black smoke high into the sky above the town.

So what did the Iraqis want from their invasion? On the face of it, their aims seemed quite limited. As early as 28 September, the Iraqi President, Saddam Hussein, declared that Iraq's territorial ambitions had already been realized, and that it would stop fighting if Iran recognized its sovereignty over the Shatt; returned to Arab control three small islands captured by the Shah in 1971; and ceased its campaign to incite Iraqis to rebel against their government. But it is generally assumed that there was a much wider, unspoken goal behind Iraq's action: nothing less than a swift and decisive blow against Iran that would actually topple the new Iranian revolutionary government.

If so, the Iraqis miscalculated badly. First, they over-estimated the chaos caused by the revolution in Iran. Instead of crumbling before the Iraqis, the Iranians absorbed their early advances while mobilizing their own resources. They were undoubtedly inspired by the resistance shown in Khorramshahr and Abadan. Secondly, the Iraqis clearly hoped that the Arab population of Khuzestan would rise up on their side and help propel them forward. They did not.

Finally, Iran is a vast country, three times bigger than Iraq. An Iraqi advance of just a few kilometres into Iranian territory was never likely to pose an immediate threat to the central government in Tehran. On the contrary, the new external threat served to unite most Iranians behind their leaders. For the Iranian leadership itself, the Iraqi assault became a test of its legitimacy. Hence, Iranian leaders, from the first, insisted that there was no question of a ceasefire until the Iraqis had been thrown back across the border.

Once the Iraqis had lost the momentum of their early

advances in the fighting around Khorramshahr and Abadan, they never regained it. Within a matter of weeks, the thoughts of both sides turned from the prospect of a decisive Iraqi blow against Iran in a classic blitzkrieg to one of a long campaign of attrition. But few observers can have predicted then that, over seven years and many hundreds of thousands of lives later, the conflict would still be raging, with little likelihood of an early end to the fighting in sight.

The Iraqi President, Saddam Hussein, took the decision to attack Iran, and the Iranians are demanding his removal from power as part of their price for ending the war.

2
'Saddam's Qadisiya'

The Gulf War has now been going for many years and there seems little prospect of a solution in the near future. In fact, the present conflict between Iran and Iraq has origins

الواقدى الابتدائية الجنيد
للبنين

The Iraqi authorities try to portray the present war as part of a historic struggle between Arabs and Persians. Here, children in Baghdad are reminded of this by scenes painted on the walls of their school.

stretching back over many centuries.

Iraq's leaders have tried to elevate the Gulf War in the minds of their people to the status of the latest episode in a historic struggle between the Arabs and the Persians which has gone on since the seventh century. The Iraqis constantly evoke the image of the Battle of Qadisiya which took place in AD 637. It was at Qadisiya that the newly founded Arab Muslim caliphate decisively defeated the Persians. At the time, the Arabs were heavily outnumbered (just as the Iraqis are today) but years of war and internal strife had weakened the power of the Persian Empire, and the Arabs succeeded in destroying it. Now, in Iraq, the Gulf War is referred to as 'Saddam's Qadisiya'.

The modern states of Iraq and Iran were created out of empires which had been struggling against each other for centuries.

The Religious Split

As the Arabs completed their historic conquest of the Persians, the seeds of the religious aspect of the Gulf War were being sown – the bitter split between Sunni and Shi'a Muslims. The founder of the Muslim religion, the prophet Muhammad, died in AD 632 leaving no successors. The rival claimants to the succession were Muhammad's father-in-law Abu Bakr, and his son-in-law, Ali. It was Abu Bakr who won acceptance as 'caliph' (successor to the prophet), but he died within two years. Ali continued to vie for power with Abu Bakr's successors, with strong support from Iraq and the east of the new Arab empire. He almost succceeded but was further opposed by the powerful Ummayyad family, who ruled Syria. When Ali met his death in 661, the Ummayyads were victorious and they established a caliphate in Damascus which was to dominate the Arab empire for nearly a century.

Those Muslims who support the Ummayyad line of succession have come to be known as Sunnis, and numerically they are now overwhelmingly dominant in Islam. But, even after the deaths of Ali and his son, Hussein, their supporters, who came to be called Shi'a, remained strong in the east of the empire. The legacy of this is that today the Shi'a are in a majority not just in Iran, but also amongst the Arabs of Iraq. Indeed, the Shi'a holy cities of Najaf and Kerbala, on the sites where Ali and Hussein died, are both within modern Iraq. But only in Iran has there been a tradition of the Shi'a actually holding power, and this is at the heart of the religious conflict now between Iraq and Iran.

In AD 750, the eastern tribes of the Arab empire finally overthrew the Ummayyad dynasty, to establish the Abbasid Caliphate, with Baghdad as its capital. It was to develop into a great civilization – the inspiration for 'The One Thousand and One Nights' – and, ironically, the conquered Persians were to become increasingly influential in it.

Iranian women, clad in traditional Islamic dress, demonstrating their support for the Iranian revolution.

19

There then followed a period of decline and, in the thirteenth century, new invaders came from the east, in the form of the Mongols led by the great Genghis Khan. The Mongol conquest heralded more than two centuries of stagnation. But, in the early sixteenth century a new Persian empire emerged under Ismail Safavi, who made himself Shah. It was he who established Shi'ism as the state religion in Persia.

But, as the Safavid empire grew, it came up against the eastward advance of a strong new Sunni Muslim power, the Ottoman Empire. A bitter struggle ensued until the two powers signed a border agreement in 1639, with the Ottomans in control of most of what is now Iraq.

However, the agreement did not define the border precisely and tension persisted between the two powers, breaking out again into open war in 1821.

Treaties of Erzerum

The general border arrangement was reaffirmed by the 1823 Treaty of Erzerum. But still the tensions remained, and began to revolve increasingly around the issue of control of the vital Shatt al-Arab waterway, formed by the confluence of the Tigris, Euphrates, and Karun rivers before they empty into the Gulf. By now, the Great Powers were taking an interest in the dispute. Britain, in particular, feared that a renewed war between the Ottomans and the Persians might be exploited by its imperial rival, Russia, which had

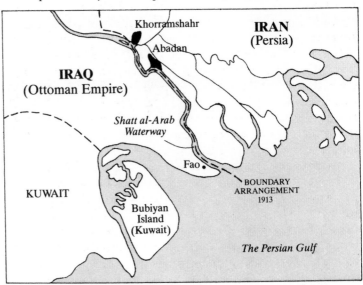

One of the main areas of tension between Iraq and Iran has long been their disputed southern boundary along the strategic Shatt al-Arab waterway.

common borders with both powers. And, with the coming of steamships, there was also the question of commercial exploitation of the Shatt.

So, a border commission was set up in 1843, with representatives from Britain, Russia, the Ottoman Empire, and Persia. And the ensuing Second Treaty of Erzerum in 1847 appeared to give control of the Shatt to the Ottomans, with the border designated as the east bank of the waterway. Then, in 1913, the Constantinople Protocol between the same four powers confirmed that judgement, while setting out the border demarcation in much greater detail.

The Persians were clearly unhappy with the arrangement over the Shatt, which they felt had been unjustly imposed on them by the Great Powers. They might have been able to redress the situation in their favour when the Ottoman Empire collapsed in the First World War, but the British occupied Iraq and were granted a mandate over the country in 1920. It was only when Iraq became independent in 1932 that Iran had a realistic opportunity to challenge Iraqi control of the Shatt. Yet, even then, the 1937 treaty negotiated between the two countries made only minor concessions in the Persians' favour.

Since the Second World War, the modern states of Iraq and Iran have increasingly vied with each other for regional dominance in the Gulf. And control of the Shatt al-Arab waterway has continued to be the main focus of their rivalry. For Iran, especially, the development of its port of Khorramshahr and the oil refinery at Abadan substantially increased the Shatt's economic importance.

Between the end of the Second World War and the mid-1970s, the balance of power between Iraq and Iran seemed to swing decisively in the latter's favour. First, Iraq was weakened by repeated political upheavals. In 1958, the Hashemite monarchy was overthrown in a bloody military coup d'etat. Three further coups followed before the socialist Ba'ath Party, which is still in power today, took control. Secondly, the Iraqi authorities faced serious unrest amongst their Kurdish minority in the north, which was struggling for greater autonomy, and which received substantial support from the Iranians. And finally, when Britain announced its intention to withdraw from the Gulf in 1968, the British and, more importantly, the Americans, made it clear that they would be looking to Iran to take on the role of dominant power in the region. In the light of the Western

One of the first and most lasting casualties in the Gulf War has been Iraqi and Iranian shipping. The Shatt-al-Arab waterway has been blocked throughout the entire conflict. Here, vessels lie devastated at the Iranian port of Khorramshahr, destroyed by Iraqi shelling.

support and military assistance to Iran which followed, Iraq's improving relations with the USSR hardly amounted to an adequate counterweight.

The course of the two countries' dispute over the Shatt illustrates how the balance of power between them shifted towards Iran up to the mid-1970s. First, on 16 February 1961, Iran announced that henceforth vessels using its ports would be guided by Iranian pilots, rather than Iraqis, as hitherto. In response, the Iraqi pilots went on strike, and traffic in the waterway came to a standstill. Iran was forced to back down.

But the dispute was revived in 1969, and this time Iraq was the instigator. The Iraqis, no doubt in an attempt to reassert their authority over Iran, forbade any vessel using the Shatt from flying the Iranian flag. They also revived historic calls for greater autonomy for the ethnic Arab population of the southern Iranian border province of Khuzestan, which they provocatively dubbed 'Arabistan'.

The Iranian response this time was to declare the 1937 border treaty null and void. In its place, they enforced the arrangement they had always favoured for the waterway, placing the frontier on the thalweg, or middle line, of the channel, rather than on its east bank. And, on this occasion, Iran had the naval and military power to support its move. The Iraqis, already heavily engaged in fighting the Kurds, were not prepared to confront the Iranians as well.

Iran added insult to Iraq's injury by occupying the Arab islands of Abu Musa and the two Tunbs in the lower Gulf in November 1971; the Iraqis were powerless to respond, and the action appeared to underline Iran's position as the dominant Gulf power. And, finally, Iran's victory over Iraq appeared to be sealed when, at a meeting of the Organization of Petroleum Exporting Countries (OPEC) in Algiers in

The last Shah and Empress of Iran. The Shah and his family were forced to flee the country as opposition to his rule mounted, paving the way for the establishment of the Islamic republic.

23

March 1975, the Iraqi Vice-President, Saddam Hussein, and the Shah of Iran concluded an agreement whereby Iraq accepted the new border arrangement along the Shatt in return for an Iranian undertaking to stop support for Iraqi Kurds fighting the government in Baghdad.

Of course, the 1975 Algiers Agreement did not end the rivalry between Iraq and Iran. The only difference now was that it was Iraq that was the aggrieved party.

It was the events of 1979 that were finally to set Iraq and Iran on the path to war. First, in February, the Shah of Iran was overthrown, and Iran became a Shi'a Islamic Republic with Ayatollah Khomeini at its head. Khomeini had a particular reason to be bitter towards the Iraqis, because just a few months earlier they had thrown him out of Iraq after 15 years of exile in the holy city of Najaf, as a goodwill gesture to the Shah. The second significant event of 1979 was the coming to power in Iraq of a ruthless and ambitious new leader in the person of Saddam Hussein.

Relations between Iraq and Iran quickly deteriorated. Iran's new religious leaders began to speak openly of exporting their revolution, and they started a campaign to incite Iraq's Shi'a community to rebel against the country's Sunni leadership. There was serious unrest amongst Iraqi Shi'as, and on 1 April 1980, there was an Iranian-backed attempt on the life of the Iraqi Deputy Prime Minister, and one of Saddam's closest associates, Tariq Aziz. The Iraqis responded with widespread arrests and deportations of Shi'a of Iranian origin.

Armed clashes were by now occurring along the entire length of the Iraqi–Iranian border. And these escalated into border artillery duels, and even air strikes. Finally, on 4 and 7 September 1980, Iraq accused Iran of shelling border towns from territory which it said should have been handed over to Iraq as part of the Algiers Agreement.

Whether or not these actions amounted to acts of war, the Iraqi leadership clearly felt threatened by the new militant Islamic government in Tehran, and probably felt that some form of conflict between the two countries was inevitable. Given this background, they apparently concluded that perhaps the time was right, with Iran still in turmoil and weakened after its revolution, to 'teach the Iranians a lesson'. On 17 September, the Iraqis declared that Iranian actions meant that the 1975 Algiers Agreement was no longer operative, and, within six days, their invasion of Iran was under way.

3
Iran's Human Waves

Once Iraq's initial advance had faltered, the fighting between the two sides died down for several months, except for a few minor operations. But both sides, and particularly the Iranians, used the time to rebuild their forces. Indeed, as

The Iranian armed forces were in a poor state when Iraq invaded. But they were able to reorganize and eventually push the Iraqis back across the border.

well as regrouping their army, the Iranians began a massive mobilization to strengthen their revolutionary militia, the Pasdaran, and recruit a new force, the Baseej, a mass movement of volunteer youths with the minimum of military

training and little more than their Islamic faith and fervour to carry them into battle. The Baseej in particular were to suffer grievously as the Iranians pushed the Iraqis back across the border.

The Iranian town of Susangerd suffered greatly during several months of siege.

The Islamic republic established a new militia, the Pasdaran, which has increasingly taken over from the regular armed forces as Iran's main fighting force.

After eight months of minor skirmishing, the Iranians launched a counter-attack in May 1981 to dislodge the Iraqis from positions that they held outside the town of Susangerd. Then there was another lull until late September, when, in several days of heavy fighting, the Iranians were able to lift the siege of Abadan, which was a great boost to their morale.

In November came their biggest operation to date, the recapture of Bostan. This was notable also because it was the first time that they employed the 'human wave' tactic.

Youngsters, some barely teenagers, were flung into battle with hardly any weapons. Their sheer numbers and their religious and revolutionary ardour were supposed to overcome Iraq's superior firepower.

Iran Regains Khorramshar

The tactic succeeded, but only at enormous cost. Iran launched several major offensives against the Iraqis in Khuzestan between March and May 1982. And it soon became clear that the Iraqi troops had little stomach for fighting a determined foe on foreign soil. Thousands surrendered in the face of the Iranian onslaught, and were taken prisoner.

So the Iranians prepared to retake Khorramshahr. They amassed a force of some 70,000 men for the assault, which began on 20 May. In fact, the occupying Iraqis put up little resistance. Back in Baghdad, Saddam Hussein, who had seen his vision of a quick victory over Iran long since evaporate, feared the political consequences of heavy Iraqi casualties. So the Iraqi army withdrew from Khorramshahr after just four days of fighting, although not without leaving behind large amounts of equipment and, again, many prisoners.

The Iraqis are short of manpower compared to Iran, but compensate by having better equipment. An Iraqi soldier with a bazooka in positions near Abadan.

Opposite *The Iranians have even had children fighting on their side. Here, a twelve-year-old boy stands guard over Iraqi prisoners of war.*

Iraq on the Defensive

The Iraqis' adventure into Iran had by now turned very sour for them, and not just on the battlefront. The Iraqi economy was also now under very great strain. At the beginning of the war Iraq, thanks to its earnings from the 1970s oil boom, had accumulated financial reserves of about $35,000 million. But, in the early days of the war, the Iranian air force swooped on Iraq's major oil installations in the south, at Fao, Mina al-Bakr, and Khor al-Amayah, and destroyed them. They also effectively blockaded Iraq's Gulf coastline. So, from the outset of the war, Iraq lost its most important oil export outlets.

In spite of this, and the fact that they now had to pay for the war, the Iraqis continued with a major development programme. Clearly this 'guns and butter' policy could not continue indefinitely, and when, in April 1982, Iraq's arch enemy in the Arab world, Syria, cut off another important Iraqi oil export pipeline which ran through Syrian territory, the Iraqi economy seemed on the verge of crisis. The Iraqis were only able to survive economically by cutting back drastically on their development plans, running up large debts with their trading partners, and calling on massive financial aid from their Gulf Arab neighbours.

Against this background, Iraq announced in June 1982 that its forces were pulling out of Iran. The hope was clearly that Iran would agree to stop fighting. It did not. For the Iranians, it was now not enough just to expel the Iraqis from their territory; they were now demanding that, as they put it, the aggressor must be punished, Saddam Hussein and his government must be removed, and Iran must be paid reparations of at least $150,000 million.

To accompany their new tougher stand, the Iranians launched their first offensive actually into Iraqi territory in July. They threw at least 100,000 men against Iraq's second city of Basra, near the southern border. But the Iraqis had prepared their defences well this time. The Iranians also found that fighting the Iraqis on their own territory was a very different proposition from fighting them in Iran. And, finally, a lot of experienced Iranian personnel had by now melted back into civilian life, so that it was inexperienced Pasdaran and Baseej forces which bore the full brunt of the fighting. The results were perhaps predictable. The Iranians made a little headway towards Basra, but failed to make a breakthrough, and they suffered enormous casualties in the

'killing zones' which the Iraqis had created for them. Undaunted, Iran launched two more offensives further north, in October and November. They both suffered the same fate as the attack on Basra.

The fighting in 1983 followed the same pattern as that established in 1982. Only in the north did the Iranians have any real success: they captured some strategic heights in the Hajj Omran region in July 1983, and the so-called 'Penjwin salient' in October and November.

Basically, the situation was one of stalemate. But Iraq was now very much on the defensive, and the initiative in the war lay with Iran.

The Iranians have relied on popular volunteers, including women, to defend their revolution. This is a woman military instructor.

4
Iraq Under Pressure

While the Iranians now held the initiative in the war, they had made little actual progress on the ground. So the Iranian leadership began to call increasingly for a 'final blow' against Iraq. These calls led to a series of offensives which has tested Iraq's defences to the limit.

Iran's advances have had most success in the marshy areas of southern Iraq, like the Majnoon islands, where the Iraqis cannot make so much use of their superior firepower.

In February 1984, Iran launched a massive human wave offensive, involving about a quarter of a million men, on the central and southern war fronts. In fact, they failed to break through, and again suffered enormous casualties. For one thing they apparently believed, mistakenly, that the Iraqi Shi'a in the south and in the army would defect to their side, rather as the Iraqis had wrongly concluded in 1980 that the ethnic Arabs of Khuzestan would rise up to welcome them. Instead, the Iraqi Shi'a have consistently proved to be Iraqis first, and Shi'a second.

The other reason for the Iranians' lack of progress was, once again, the huge earthwork defences which the Iraqis had constructed, festooned with mines, heavy machine guns, artillery, and tanks. Indeed, the one area where the Iranians did gain some ground was in the waterlogged terrain north of

The Iranians, with inferior equipment to the Iraqis, have made up for this in part with greater ingenuity. For example, they have used large numbers of small boats, equipped with machine guns, for fighting in the Huweizah marshes north of Basra, and even for attacks on tankers in the Persian Gulf.

Basra known as the Hawizah marshes, where the Iraqis could not bring their superior firepower to bear. Here, the Iranians were able to capture and hold the Majnoon oilfield.

The main advantage for the Iraqis of their huge static defences was that it allowed them to be relatively sparing in their use of manpower. The Iraqi leadership had realized that, with a population just a third that of Iran's, they simply could not afford to take casualties on anything like the scale that Iran was suffering. That is why the Iraqis have become so reluctant to launch counterattacks against Iranian offensives, preferring instead to preserve their troop strength.

The losses that the Iranians sustained in their 1984 offensive meant that it was a year before they could launch another attack. But, in the intervening period, they made sure that they learnt the lessons of the past. They improved

their training, bought new equipment, and improved their supply lines. The regular armed forces were also brought more into the military planning again. Because of their lack of success, 1984 had seen the last of the pure human wave offensives.

It was March 1985 when the Iranians launched their next big offensive, with the apparent aim of cutting Basra off from the rest of Iraq. Superficially, the result of this offensive was much the same as those of the past, with the Iranians making little headway. But there were important warning signs for

The Iranian leadership has developed a deep sense of anti-Americanism, because of the close ties between the US and the regime of the former Shah.

Iraq in the 1985 fighting.

First, the Iranians were able to inflict heavy casualties on the Iraqis, similar in scale to those that they themselves suffered. Secondly, the Iraqis were forced to bring in substantial reinforcements from elsewhere along the war front to halt the Iranian advance. And, thirdly, the Iranians were able briefly to cut the strategic Baghdad–Basra highway, emphasizing Iraq's lack of strategic depth; the Iranians do not have to advance very far before important targets come within their grasp. Even Baghdad is only just over 120

kilometres from the frontier, whereas Tehran is nearly 500 kilometres away.

Constrained by their need to minimise casualties on the ground, the Iraqis have increasingly turned to their air force as their main instrument for carrying the war into Iran. By 1985, Iraq had a massive air superiority over Iran. The Iraqi air force had an inventory of over 300 modern combat aircraft, chiefly supplied by the USSR and France. In 1979, Iran had had a modern air force, with 75 American-made F-14 Tomcats, 120 F-4 Phantoms, and 160 F-5s. But after the revolution and the Iranian hostage crisis, in which the Iranians had held 53 US citizens to ransom in the American embassy in Tehran for 14 months, the USA imposed an arms embargo on the country. And, with the start of the Gulf War as well, many of America's allies, plus other countries, followed suit. So the Iranians found it increasingly difficult to service and maintain their aircraft, and, by 1985, they had fewer than 90 operational jets.

Iraqi air raids on Tehran and other Iranian cities and towns have caused severe damage and serious disruption. Here Iranian schoolgirls help build air-raid shelters in Tehran.

'War of the Cities'

On 10 February 1984, Iraq had launched a wave of attacks on Iranian cities, to which the Iranians had replied with artillery bombardments of a number of Iraqi border towns. The UN Secretary-General, Javier Perez De Cuellar, was able to negotiate a partial ceasefire against civilian targets on 12 June 1984. But on 4 March 1985 an Iraqi air raid on the Iranian town of Ahwaz reignited what became known as 'the war of the cities'. On 11 March, the Iraqi air force carried out the first of a long series of air raids on Tehran and other Iranian cities. Iran replied with missile attacks on Baghdad, using Soviet-designed Scud-B rockets which may have been supplied by Libya, Syria, or North Korea.

The Iraqi air raids undoubtedly caused serious disruption. But, far from undermining the Iranians' morale, the attacks seemed to stiffen their resistance. So, on 14 June, Saddam Hussein announced a unilateral two-week ceasefire in the war of the cities, supposedly to give the Iranian leadership time to reconsider its position on ending the war. In fact, Iraqi air raids on Iranian cities did not resume for over a year, and Iran too desisted from further missile attacks.

In early 1986, Iran scored perhaps its greatest success of the entire war. The Iranians launched a new offensive on 9 February with a force of over 100,000 men. The Iraqis had been expecting the attack to come in the Hawizah marshes, north of Basra, and had concentrated most of their defences there. But, during the night and under thick cloud cover, the Iranians also crossed the Shatt al-Arab waterway south of the city, and launched a surprise attack on Iraq's Fao peninsula. They quickly overcame ill-prepared Iraqi defenders, and, with their own improved preparations, were soon able to reinforce their attack and establish a major foothold in Fao that virtually cut Iraq off from its Gulf coastline. Iraq was not to recapture Fao until 1988.

The Fao offensive was a tremendous shock to Baghdad, and it also sent shudders through the region, as there were momentary fears that Iraq's defences might collapse. So, to try and regain some prestige, Saddam Hussein took the unusual step in mid-May of ordering an attack on the central front to capture the Iranian border town of Mehran. But the plan backfired; the Iranians recaptured Mehran in July.

It had been a bad six months for the Iraqis, but they were to win some redemption in the second half of the year. Since early 1984, the Iraqi air force had been carrying out a sustained campaign of attacks on Iran's oil installations and tanker traffic, and the Iraqis had virtually laid siege to Iran's Kharg Island oil terminal, in the northern Gulf, which was responsible for about four-fifths of Iran's oil exports. With tanker owners increasingly reluctant to sail to Kharg, the Iranians were forced to start a shuttle service of their own tankers to ferry the oil to transhipment facilities further down the Gulf. But, on 12 August 1986, the Iraqi air force

Civilian casualties in the war of the cities, including children, have been heavy. Here, a father mourns over the body of his daughter, a victim of an Iraqi air-raid into Iran.

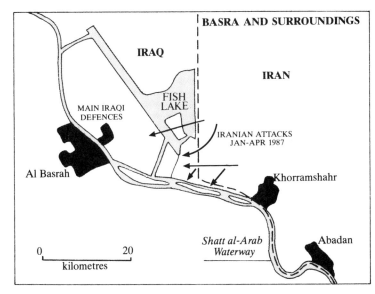

BASRA AND SURROUNDINGS

IRAQ

IRAN

FISH LAKE

MAIN IRAQI DEFENCES

IRANIAN ATTACKS JAN-APR 1987

Al Basrah

Khorramshahr

Shatt al-Arab Waterway

Abadan

0   20
kilometres

The Iranian invasion of Iraq in the early part of 1987 was thwarted mainly by Iraq's massive static defences, including the specially constructed Fish Lake.

attacked the facility at Sirri Island, damaging at least three tankers. On 5 September, it hit the southern Iranian oil terminal on Lavan Island. And, finally, on 25 November, the Iraqis damaged another three tankers at Larak Island, in the Strait of Hormuz at the very entrance to the Gulf, demonstrating their ability to hit Iranian shipping anywhere in the Gulf. The result of these attacks was that Iran's oil exports, which had been running at something over 1·5 million barrels a day, were for a time cut virtually in half.

But this did not deter the Iranians. For most of 1986, Iran's leaders had been promising a final, decisive offensive against Iraq, and by the second half of the year Western intelligence agencies were reporting a mass Iranian build-up of up to half a million men on the southern front.

For some time, the Pasdaran had been receiving preference over the regular army in terms of training and equipment. And it was the Pasdaran who were in the vanguard when the Iranians finally launched their 'decisive blow' against Iraq on 8 January 1987.

The Iranian offensive was due west towards Basra, and the onslaught was undoubtedly ferocious. The Iranians were able to advance several kilometres, and inflict heavy casualties again on the Iraqis. And with reports of thousands of people fleeing Basra, there were fears once again that Iraq's resistance would crumble, and Saddam Hussein be toppled from power.

41

But Iraq had again constructed massive static defences east of Basra, including a huge water barrier called Fish Lake. So, even though the Iranians were able to sustain their pressure for an unprecedented six weeks, and even have their regular army launch a separate offensive on the central front on 14 January to try to distract Iraq's attention, the Iraqi army did not crack. On 26 February, the Iranians announced the end of their 'decisive' offensive without achieving the desired breakthrough. The Iranians were to make several more pushes between February and April, but without any significant gains.

The Iraqi air force had played a major part in countering the Iranian attacks, mounting large numbers of sorties against Iranian positions and troop formations. From 9 January, it also once again carried out numerous air raids on Iranian cities, in response to which Iran again attacked Baghdad with Scud-B missiles. And, as the fighting for Basra subsided, the air force was to move very much into the limelight as the focus of world attention shifted from the land to the waters of the Gulf, and the so-called 'tanker war'.

At the front. Despite their enormous numbers of soldiers, the Iranian offensives have been generally unsuccessful.

5
The Kurdish Question

The Kurds are a distinct ethnic and linguistic group inhabiting a mountainous region stretching across northern
Iraq, north-western Iran, and parts of Syria, Turkey, and
the Soviet Union. Clearly, therefore, the development of
Kurdish nationalist sentiment during the twentieth century
has had implications for all these countries. But it is in Iraq
that the Kurdish fight for a measure of statehood has had
most impact, because there the Kurds constitute a significant one-fifth of the population, and are highly concentrated
in one area in the north of the country. So, not surprisingly,
the Kurdish question has threatened to have an important

*The villages of
southern Iraq,
including al-Baida
here, have taken a
heavy pounding in the
fighting.*

impact on the course of the Gulf War.

Iraq's Kurds rose in rebellion in 1961, and, from 1964, received substantial assistance from Iran. The Kurdish fighters proved very adept at warfare in the mountains of

Each side has tried to encourage unrest in the other's country. Here, members of the Iraqi-backed Iranian Mujahadeen, including Iranian Kurds and other opposition groups, are seen training in Iraqi Kurdistan.

their homeland, and the Iraqi army became bogged down in a costly war. Tentative ceasefire agreements in 1964, 1966, and 1967 all collapsed. It was not until 1970 that the Iraqi government, in the wake of its humiliation at the hands of

Iran over the Shatt al-Arab, agreed to a 15-point peace plan, which provided for Kurdish autonomy, recognition of Kurdish as an official language in the autonomous region, and proportional representation for the Kurds in a national legislative body.

But the Kurds became dissatisfied with the implementation of the agreement, and this led to renewed fighting in 1974. It was only the withdrawal of Iranian support for the Kurds as part of the 1975 Algiers Agreement that brought the fighting to an end.

Of course, the Kurds saw the outbreak of the Gulf War as a new opportunity to press for greater independence. But the rebellion in Iran was short-lived, despite Iraqi encouragement, and it has again been in Iraq that the Kurds have proved most troublesome.

Saddam Hussein clearly recognized the potential of this threat. It was he, in fact, who negotiated the 1970 agreement, and in 1984 and 1985 he attempted to negotiate another agreement with one of the Iraqi Kurdish groups, the Patriotic Union of Kurdistan (PUK), but the talks proved abortive.

Instead, the Kurds, with help from the Iranian Pasdaran, have mounted sabotage attacks and guerrilla raids against the Iraqi army in the north. And the Iranians scored a major success in December 1986 by forging an alliance between the PUK and the other main Iraqi Kurdish group, the Kurdish Democratic Party, after years of bitter rivalry. It was that that led to an increase in Kurdish activity in 1987, in response to which the Iraqi authorities adopted a tough new 'scorched earth' policy of razing large numbers of Kurdish villages and resettling their inhabitants elsewhere to try to reduce support for the guerrillas.

Nevertheless, the guerrillas control much of the countryside in north-eastern Iraq, with the government's authority often confined to the major towns. They also pose an ever-present threat to Iraq's major northern oilfield around Kirkuk, and its vital oil export pipelines and strategic highway to Turkey. So far, the Kurds have failed actually to threaten these targets directly, except for a daring raid by the PUK and some Pasdaran on the Kirkuk oil refinery on 11 October 1986, which caused minor damage. But the Iraqi government has undoubtedly had to divert substantial numbers of troops away from the war front with Iran in order to deal with the problem.

6
Fallout from the War

There are no reliable figures available for the number of casualties so far in the Gulf War. However, it is generally accepted that the death toll on both sides is at least 500,000, with many more wounded. There can be few families on either side that have not been directly affected by the war. Iraq has also seen its second city and major port, Basra, pounded throughout the war by Iranian artillery, while Iran saw its port of Khorramshahr devastated during Iraq's invasion. Baghdad has also been hit by many Scud-B missiles, and the Iraqi air force has carried out numerous air raids on Tehran and other Iranian cities.

Iraqi students helping with rebuilding work in Baghdad.

The Economic Toll

On the economic front, Basra has not functioned as a port since the beginning of the war, and Iraq's Gulf oil outlets were also rendered useless at the start of hostilities. The Iraqis were forced virtually to halt their ambitious development programme in 1982–3, yet have still amassed foreign debts of at least $50,000 million. Some $30,000 million of this has been given by the Gulf Arab states, and will probably never be repaid, but Iraq has still been forced to reschedule its debt repayments with most of its major trading partners. However, the worst may be over for the Iraqis in this respect, as they have seen new oil export pipelines come on stream through Saudi Arabia and Turkey since 1985.

In contrast to Iraq's foreign debt, Iran's seems small at $5–10,000 million. However, the Iranians have had their major oil export refinery at Abadan out of action since September 1980. There is also evidence that Iraq's campaign of attacks on Iranian economic targets, and particularly Iran's oil exports, has been having an increasingly serious effect on its economy and war effort.

Political Repercussions

Yet, at a political level, the Gulf War seems actually to have helped the governments in both countries to consolidate their positions. For Iraq's ruling Ba'ath Party, the war has been a useful pretext for toughening its authoritarian methods, and clamping down on opposition groups. Moreover, Saddam Hussein has come to personify Iraq's resistance to Iran, to which most Iraqis still seem dedicated. There are occasional signs of dissent against the government – sporadic car bombings in Baghdad by Shi'a and Kurdish elements, the more general Kurdish activity, and substantial desertions from the army – but little evidence of widely organized opposition. The president has surrounded himself with supporters and the Ba'ath Party has penetrated every national institution, including the army.

In Iran, the new Islamic republic had far from established itself when Iraq invaded in 1980, presenting the Iranian leaders with a clear external threat around which to unite their people. Since then, the growth of the Pasdaran has provided the leadership with a powerful instrument of support. It has been widely argued that, had the Iraqis restrained themselves in 1980, they would have seen the Islamic republic collapse by itself.

Opposite A huge cult has developed around the personality of the Iraqi President, Saddam Hussein, who has come to personify Iraq's resistance to Iran. This is one of thousands of portraits of the president, usually depicting him in a war-like pose, which are seen throughout Iraq.

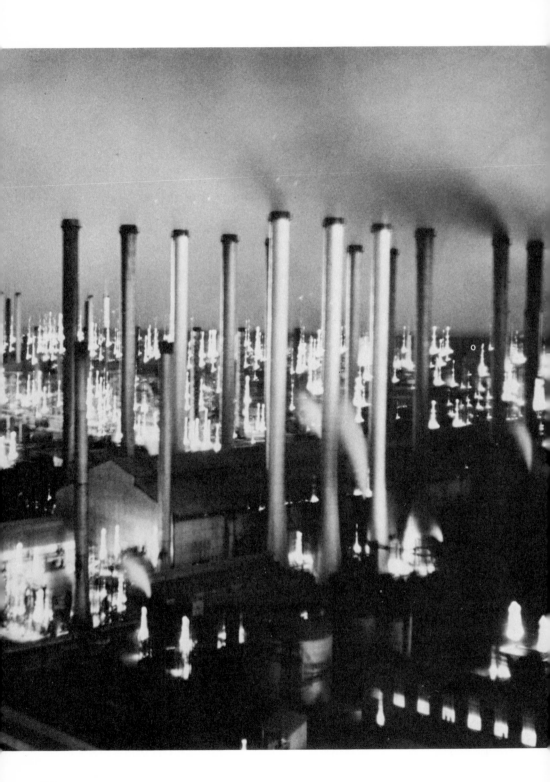

The Gulf Co-operation Council

The Gulf War has, of course, always had the potential to spill over to involve the Gulf Arab states. In the past, the Gulf Arabs were as suspicious of Iraq's regional ambitions as they were of Iran's. It was, after all, Iraq which laid claim to Kuwait in 1961. The ruling families in the Gulf were also concerned about the socialist ideology of Iraq's Ba'ath Party. But, since 1979, the prospect of an Iranian-led Shi'a Islamic revolution sweeping through the Gulf has been seen by the Sunni-dominated governments in the Arab states as by far the greater threat. Hence, they have backed Iraq in the Gulf War as a bulwark against such a development. But this fact has simply combined with the fundamental religious animosity to provoke a growing antagonism between Iran and the Gulf Arab states during the course of the war.

Kuwait has been the main target for Iranian anger, because of its particularly strong support for Iraq. Kuwait has been the victim of a number of Iranian-inspired bomb outrages, the most serious being an attempt on the life of the Emir in May 1985. Iran has also paid particular attention in its shipping attacks to vessels trading with Kuwait, and in 1987 fired over half a dozen Chinese-made Silkworm missiles at Kuwait. Meanwhile, in June 1984, the Saudi air force had shot down an Iranian Phantom apparently preparing to attack Saudi Arabia's Ras Tanura oil terminal. Most seriously of all, over 400 pilgrims, mainly Iranian, were killed on 31 July 1987 during the annual pilgrimage, or *Hajj*, to Makkah in Saudi Arabia. The Iranians charged the Saudi security forces with shooting the pilgrims, while the Saudis insisted they had died in a stampede sparked-off by an illegal Iranian demonstration.

On 25 May 1981, the six Gulf Arab states – Saudi Arabia, Kuwait, Oman, the United Arab Emirates (UAE), Qatar, and Bahrain – formed the Gulf Co-operation Council (GCC). All the GCC states have since invested heavily in bolstering their defences, and have also between themselves formed a joint force, the Peninsula Shield.

However, between them, the GCC states have a population of just 12 million, compared to Iran's 50 million, and armed forces of only 160,000. Hence, they have been forced to search for assistance elsewhere to guard against a major Iranian threat.

That was undoubtedly the motive behind the decision of five of the GCC states in November 1987 to restore diplo-

Opposite The refinery at Shuaiba, in the oil-rich state of Kuwait. The Kuwaitis have suffered a number of attacks by Iran, because of their strong support for Iraq. It is strongly suspected that Iran was involved in the hijack of a Kuwaiti plane in 1988 in which members of the Kuwaiti royal family were held hostage for many days.

The coffins of those killed at Makkah on 31 July, 1987, are carried by the angry crowd in Tehran.

matic relations with Egypt, which they had severed in 1979 in protest at Egypt's peace treaty with Israel (Oman never broke its relations). Egypt, with a population of 52 million, and over half a million men under arms, is the only Arab state other than Iraq that can pose as a realistic counterweight to Iran. The Arab world also increased its

efforts to persuade Iran's main Arab backer, Syria, to reconcile with Iraq. Syria and Iraq have long been rivals in the Arab world, there are opposing arms of the *Ba'ath* Party in power in each country, and President Hafez al-Assad of Syria and Saddam Hussein are believed to dislike each other personally. So, when Iraq invaded Iran, Syria sided with Iran.

Superpower Involvement

However, the most significant development of 1987 was probably Kuwait's decision to call on the superpowers to help protect its shipping from Iranian attack.

The Persian Gulf has increasingly become a region of superpower competition. Its strategic significance lies in its oil wealth. In the 1970s, a quarter of all American and two-thirds of European and Japanese oil imports came from the Gulf. The oil glut of the 1980s has reduced this dependence temporarily, but Gulf oil will grow in importance again as marginal oil exporters like Britain leave the scene in the 1990s.

US President Jimmy Carter, in his State of the Union Address on 23 January 1980, declared that 'any attempt by any outside power to gain control of the Persian Gulf region

US President Jimmy Carter. It was he who first announced a major American military commitment to the Gulf, in the wake of the Iranian revolution, because of fears over Western oil supplies.

53

As part of a general defence build-up in the Gulf, Saudi Arabia bought advanced AWACS radar warning planes from the US in 1981. But the controversy surrounding these and other American military sales in the Gulf has greatly complicated American relations with the region.

will be regarded as an assault on the vital interests of the USA and such an assault will be repelled by any means necessary, including military force'. The great fear in Washington at the time was that the USSR would take advantage of the chaos in Iran following the fall of the Shah to move into that country, and from there threaten the pro-Western states in the rest of the Gulf. The Soviet invasion of Afghanistan at the end of 1979 had greatly increased that fear, and led President Carter's National Security Adviser, Zbigniew Brzezinski, to characterise the Gulf as an 'arc of crisis'. Since the start of the war, US officials have continued to worry that the USSR might exploit the instability in the region, but they have also had to contend with the possibility of another power apparently hostile to the West, in the shape of Iran, threatening the West's oil supplies.

The USA's initial response was to create the Rapid Deployment Force of nearly 300,000 men, intended specifically for operations in the Gulf in an emergency. The Americans also deployed AWACS radar warning planes to Saudi Arabia in October 1980, pending the delivery of the Saudis' own AWACSs, and they undertook to sell substantial amounts of weaponry to the GCC states.

54

But, in 1981, the pro-Israeli lobby in the US Congress nearly blocked the sale of AWACS aircraft to Saudi Arabia, and it did succeed in halting an important sale of F-15 fighters to the same country in 1985. Such embarrassments over arms sales, plus general Arab disquiet over US policy in the Middle East, actually helped the USSR to extend its influence in the Gulf. The most tangible evidence of this came in 1985, with the decisions by Oman and the UAE to establish diplomatic relations with Moscow. Then, in November 1986, in what became known as the 'Irangate scandal', it was revealed that the USA, in direct contravention of official American policy, had sold arms to Iran to try to win the release of American hostages held by pro-Iranian groups in Lebanon.

Hence, US President Ronald Reagan's decision in 1987 to 'reflag' eleven Kuwaiti tankers, and provide them with a US Navy escort, had three motives: to protect freedom of navigation in the Gulf; to restore America's credibility amongst the Gulf Arab states as a good ally in the wake of the Irangate scandal; and to forestall further Soviet diplomatic successes in the region. However, the consequent massive American naval build-up in the Gulf immediately threatened a serious confrontation between the USA and Iran. It also raised tensions with Moscow, and it remained unclear how the Soviet leadership would react if the USA were to become involved militarily actually inside Iran, which has a long common border with the USSR.

President Reagan's critics also contrasted America's ever-worsening relations with Tehran with the USSR's apparent ability to be Iraq's major arms supplier and to woo the Gulf Arab states on the one hand, and yet maintain good relations with Iran on the other. Soviet ministers were almost monthly visitors to Tehran in 1987, and the two countries concluded several important economic agreements. The Administration's critics pointed out that, for all its hostility to the USA, Iran remained a strategically important country, because of its position, size, and wealth, and one in which the USA could not allow the USSR a free hand.

However, there was little evidence that Moscow's superficially good relations with Tehran had given it any real influence there. In 1983, the USSR had seen the Iranian communist party, the Tudeh, crushed, and 18 Soviet diplomats expelled. The Iranians have stopped and searched Soviet vessels entering the Gulf, and attacked one of them in

May 1987. The Soviets have also been unable to extract any change from the Iranians in their position on ending the Gulf War. Therefore, the prospect of a rampant Islamic republic of Iran remains as alarming for the USSR as it does for the West, because of the large number of Muslims living just across the border from Iran in Soviet Central Asia.

In view of this, and the fact that Iraq now appears to have little chance of defeating Iran militarily, the ideal solution to the Gulf War for both superpowers would appear to be a 'no victor, no vanquished' situation which at least left the political structures in both Iraq and Iran intact, and hence not susceptible to exploitation by either the USA or the USSR, and more or less preserved the balance of power in the Gulf as a whole. However, the superpowers have been unable to co-operate successfully to achieve such a favourable outcome.

The Bridgeton *was in the first convoy of reflagged Kuwaiti tankers escorted through the Gulf by the US Navy. Unfortunately for the Kuwaitis and Americans, it struck a mine as it approached Kuwaiti waters, but was hardly damaged.*

7
The Tanker War

It is in the tanker war that the greatest risk exists of outside involvement in the fighting in the Gulf. Indeed, Iraq's leaders instigated it in early 1984 with the specific hope of 'internationalizing' their conflict with Iran, and thereby hastening its end.

On 9 October 1983, the Iraqis took delivery of the weapons that they needed to execute the tanker war: French-made Super Etendard strike aircraft armed with Exocet anti-ship missiles. The first Iraqi tanker attack using Super Etendards came on 27 March 1984, and Iran's first response came on 13 May, with an attack on a Kuwaiti-owned ship.

There have been hundreds of Iraqi and Iranian attacks on shipping in the tanker war. As these attacks spread throughout the Gulf, they prompted a number of foreign countries to send warships to the area. Here a Saudi tanker, the Al-Ahood, *has been set ablaze.*

Opposite *The
Americans have had a
small naval presence
in the Gulf for over 40
years. However, after
the attack on the USS
Stark, they greatly
increased the
number of warships
in the area. Here,
the battleship USS
Missouri (left) sails
with other American
warships near the
Gulf.*

Below *The Iraqis
have generally
attacked only vessels
trading with Iran.
But, because Iraqi
shipping has been
blockaded since the
beginning of the war,
the Iranians have hit
at the ships of the
other Arab states in
the Gulf.*

By early 1987, there had been over 300 attacks on ships in the Gulf, and some 200 seamen had lost their lives. But the response of the international community was minimal. Quite simply, in spite of the level of attacks, Gulf oil supplies remained relatively unhindered and, with the general world glut of oil, the tanker war did not produce the expected oil crisis.

Then, in early 1987, Kuwait, which had seen 45 ships trading with it hit by Iran, called on the superpowers for help. In March, it was revealed that the Kuwaitis would charter three Soviet oil tankers, which would receive Soviet naval protection. In response, the USA agreed to reflag half the Kuwaiti tanker fleet under the Stars and Stripes, and provide them with a US Navy escort.

USS Stark

On 17 May, an Iraqi aircraft accidentally attacked the American frigate USS *Stark* with two Exocets, crippling it and killing 37 American sailors. The incident underlined the potential risks of the escort operation, and the American response was to increase its Gulf naval force from seven to over a dozen warships, and station an aircraft carrier task force and a battleship task force at the entrance to the Gulf. These moves led to mounting tension between the USA and

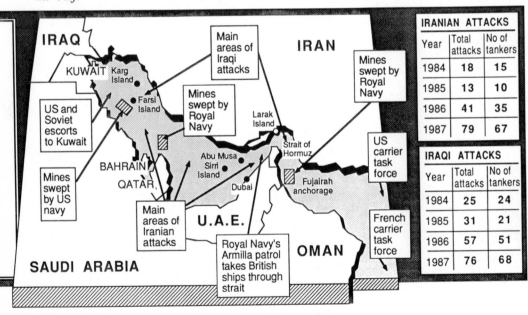

IRANIAN ATTACKS		
Year	Total attacks	No of tankers
1984	18	15
1985	13	10
1986	41	35
1987	79	67

IRAQI ATTACKS		
Year	Total attacks	No of tankers
1984	25	24
1985	31	21
1986	57	51
1987	76	68

Iran. Compared to the American build-up, the Soviet Gulf naval presence of just two destroyers and three mine-sweepers appeared tiny.

As one pretext for its naval build-up, the USA argued that the risk to shipping in the Gulf had increased because Iran

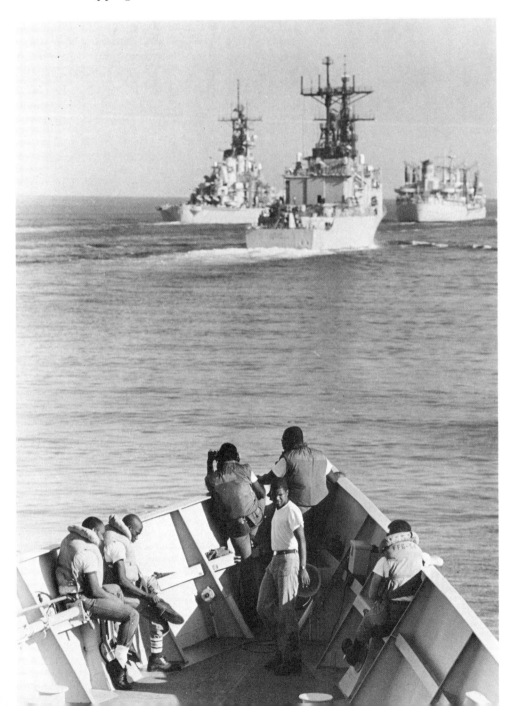

had stationed Chinese-made Silkworm anti-ship missiles near the Strait of Hormuz and on the Fao Peninsula. During 1987, the Pasdaran also began using high-speed launches to attack ships.

In spite of the escalation by Iran, and pressure from the Reagan Administration, the USA's allies were reluctant to join its reflagging operation. However, when, on 7 August, a tanker hit a mine in the Gulf of Oman, outside the Persian Gulf itself, Britain and France both agreed to boost their small naval flotillas in the area with a force of minesweepers. Italy, the Netherlands, and Belgium also later sent warships.

Mines aboard the captured Iranian warship Iran Ajr. *In the background is a warship from the US Navy's Gulf Force.*

However, the various foreign navies were meant only to protect shipping from their own countries. That left many unescorted ships sailing the Gulf. Hence, far from the foreign naval presence deterring the tanker war, well over 150 ships were attacked in 1987, more than in any previous year. So, the risk remains of a clash between Iran and one of the foreign navies, especially the US Navy.

Ironically, Iraq has attacked more ships in the tanker war than Iran. But it is the Iranians who are seen as the main threat to freedom of navigation in the Gulf. This is because Iraq has tended only to attack ships trading directly with Iran, which are generally regarded as legitimate targets,

IRAQ

Al Basrah

KUWAIT

Mina
Al-Ahmadi

Kharg
Island

IRAN

THE PERSIAN GULF

Ras Tanura

Larak
Island

Strait of Hormuz

BAHRAIN

■ Riyadh

ROSTAM
OIL PLATFORM

Sirri
Island

OMAN

Abu Musa
Island

QATAR

SAUDI ARABIA

OMAN

UNITED ARAB EMIRATES

*A map showing the
Persian Gulf*

whereas Iran, with Iraq's own shipping blockaded since 1980, has had to resort to retaliation against vessels trading with the Gulf Arab states, and this is generally regarded as neutral shipping, deserving of protection.

Rostam Oil Platform Destroyed

Both the USA and the USSR suffered early embarrassments in the escort operations. On 8 May 1987, the Soviet tanker *Ivan Koroteyev* hit a mine, apparently laid by Iran, while approaching Kuwait, and the reflagged Kuwaiti tanker *Bridgeton* did the same on 24 July. After that, incidents between the US Navy and Iran became more serious. On 21

September, the Americans attacked and captured the Iranian landing ship *Iran Ajr* while it was laying mines; several Iranians were killed. Then, on 9 October, US Navy helicopters attacked and destroyed three Iranian gunboats, after being fired on themselves. And finally, on 19 October, four US Navy destroyers shelled Iran's Rostam offshore oil platform, saying it was a Pasdaran naval base, in retaliation for two Iranian missile attacks the previous week on American tankers in Kuwaiti waters.

Kuwait's Sea Island offshore oil loading platform, which was hit by an Iranian missile in October 1987, just days after the US Navy had destroyed an Iranian platform in the lower Gulf.

8
An Elusive Peace

International Mediation

It was mounting concern about an escalation of the Gulf War which prompted the UN Security Council to pass resolution 598 on 20 July 1987, demanding an end to the conflict. For the first time, the five permanent members of the Council – the USA, the USSR, Britain, France, and China – all agreed to vote for a mandatory resolution which carried with it the threat of possible sanctions, especially an arms embargo, against whichever party did not accept it.

Iranian children taking part in a parade in Tehran. They are carrying a model of a missile. The Iranians have made considerable use of missiles to attack Baghdad.

From the outset of hostilities, a number of international bodies have tried to bring an end to the Gulf War. On 28 September 1980, President Zia ul-Haq of Pakistan led a goodwill mission to both Iran and Iraq on behalf of the Islamic Conference Organization (ICO). But the mission failed, and, after leaving Tehran, President Zia declared 'Iran is still in a revolutionary stage when conciliation and mediation do not work'. The Arab League and the GCC have also attempted peace initiatives, as have a number of individual countries, but without success.

Conditions for Peace
As the balance of advantage in the war has tilted away from Iraq, so Iraq's conditions for ending the conflict have been moderated. On 2 August 1986 President Saddam Hussein, in an open letter to Iran, offered peace on the basis of a cease-fire, a withdrawal of forces to internationally recognized borders, an exchange of prisoners, negotiations on a final settlement, and a non-aggression pact. These conditions

were close to the UN resolutions on the conflict at that time. Iraq's main stipulation was that it refused to consider partial ceasefires, such as in the tanker war, because it said that these favour Iran; as President Hussein put it, Iraq offered 'comprehensive peace or comprehensive war'.

In contrast to Iraq, Iran's war demands have increased during the course of the war to include the identification of Iraq as the aggressor (Iraq maintains that it was Iranian provocation, not Iraq's invasion, which started the war), the overthrow of Saddam Hussein and his government, and the payment to Iran of massive reparations. For Iran, given the level of its sacrifice in the fighting, the conflict with Iraq has become a *jihad*, or holy war, admitting no compromise. It is seen as a test of the country's Islamic credentials. There has been speculation that Iran's dedication to the conflict will diminish once Ayatollah Khomeini, who is 86 years old, leaves the scene. However, part of the *raison d'être* of the Iranian republic is to spread its Islamic revolution. And the level of rhetoric emanating from Khomeini's would-be successors suggests that there is still strong support for the war in Iran, particularly amongst the Pasdaran, and that this is likely to remain the case as long as the Iranians believe they have a chance of victory.

Of course, most hopes for a negotiated settlement of the Gulf War have rested with the United Nations. But the UN Security Council's first resolution on the war, passed on 28 September 1980, spoke only of the need for a ceasefire, with no hint of a need for Iraq to withdraw its forces from Iran. Ever since, Iran has regarded the Council as hopelessly biased in favour of Iraq. Even when the Security Council condemned Iraqi use of chemical weapons on 21 March 1986, Iran complained that this was too little, too late.

On 20–24 November 1980, the former Swedish Prime Minister, Olof Palme, visited Baghdad and Tehran as the UN Secretary-General's special envoy, and made a number of subsequent trips to both countries, but without achieving a ceasefire. The UN Secretary-General, Javier Perez De Cuellar, gained some limited success by negotiating a temporary ceasefire on civilian targets in June 1984, but a general peace initiative by him in April 1985 failed.

Resolution 598 of July 1987 appeared to be something of a breakthrough because, for the first time, the Security Council voted unanimously for a mandatory resolution on the war. It called for a ceasefire and a withdrawal of forces as

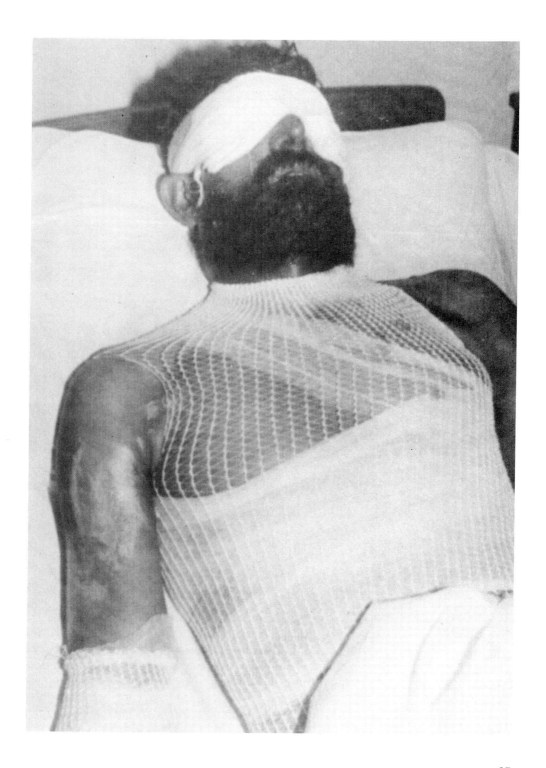

UN experts approaching an alleged Iraqi chemical bomb which has failed to explode. In March 1987 the Security Council condemned Iraq for using such weapons.

a first step, an exchange of prisoners, and mediation on a final settlement. Iraq accepted it immediately. The Security Council also tried to make the resolution attractive to Iran, by again condemning the use of chemical weapons, and proposing an impartial body to inquire into responsibility for the conflict and international assistance for reconstruction work to make good the damage caused by the fighting. However, Iran neither accepted nor rejected the resolution.

Stalemate

The Western permanent members of the Security Council immediately called for sanctions against Iran, for failing to give an unequivocal reply to the resolution. However, the Soviet Union, attempting to preserve its hard-won links with Iran, insisted that it should be given more time to accept it. Perez De Cuellar held negotiations in Baghdad and Tehran on 11–14 November, and had further contacts with the Iranians and Iraqis in New York. However, the positions of the two sides appeared immoveable and irreconcilable: Iraq demanded that the resolution be implemented precisely as it had originally been passed, while Iran insisted on Iraq being named the aggressor, and reparations being paid to Iran before any permanent ceasefire. As the months dragged by, the USSR came under increasing pressure to allow work to start on imposing an arms embargo on Iran.

The UN Secretary-General, Javier Perez De Cuellar, has had some success in negotiating limited, temporary ceasefires between Iran and Iraq, but has so far failed to negotiate an end to the conflict.

9
The Future

The Gulf War has been going on for many years now and the prospects for a negotiated settlement still appear slim. Even if the UN can agree on an arms embargo against Iran, that is unlikely to bring an early end to the fighting, as Iran has already had to contend with partial arms embargoes since

Martyrs' cemetery in Tehran. The Gulf War has already claimed very high casualties on both sides, and this looks like continuing for the foreseeable future.

the beginning of the war, and has managed to circumvent them. Moreover, tougher action by the international community to impose a settlement can be virtually ruled out.

The most likely future pattern for the war appears to be a continuation of the existing cycle of activity: periodic major Iranian offensives, with Iraq continuing to raid Iran's oil exports. Of the two belligerents, Iran now has the greater chance of victory, but neither side appears capable of inflicting decisive defeat on the other in the near future. The increased foreign naval presence in the Gulf has undoubtedly increased the risk that the conflict might spread. However, perhaps the most likely scenario is that, with increasing war weariness on both sides, the level of hostilities between them will eventually die down to a *de facto* ceasefire.

Date chart

637   Battle of Qadisiya.
750   Collapse of Ummayyad Caliphate.
1258   Destruction of Abbasid Caliphate.
1639   Persian–Ottoman boundary agreement.
1823   First Treaty of Erzerum.
1847   Second Treaty of Erzerum.
1913   Constantinople Protocol.
1932   Iraqi independence.
1937   Iraqi–Iranian border treaty.
1961   Iraqi–Iranian dispute on pilotage on Shatt al-Arab waterway.
1968   Ba'ath Party seizure of power in Iraq.
1969   Iran imposes thalweg boundary in Shatt al-Arab.
1975   Algiers Agreement.
1979   Fall of Shah of Iran. Ayatollah Khomeini seizes power, creates Islamic republic in Iran. Saddam Hussein becomes president in Iraq.
1980   Mounting border clashes between Iran and Iraq. Iraq invades Iran.
1982   Iran pushes Iraq back across border, moves into Iraq. Start of human wave offensives.
1984   Iran occupies Majnoon oilfield in Hawizah Marshes. First war of the cities. Start of tanker war. Saudi Arabia shoots down Iranian fighter.
1985   Iran briefly cuts Baghdad—Basra highway. Second war of the cities.
1986   Iran occupies Fao Peninsula. Iraq takes, then loses Mehran. Iraq attacks Iranian oil export facilities in southern Gulf.
1987   Massive Iranian offensive against Basra. USA and USSR begin protecting Kuwaiti shipping. USS *Stark* crippled by Iraqi missiles. UN resolution 598 demands end to Gulf War.
1988   Fighting in north-eastern Iraq. New outbreak of 'war of the cities'. Iraq regains Fao peninsula. US Navy blows up Sassan oil platform, sinks the Iranian frigate, *Sahand*, and cripples another, the *Sabalan*.

Glossary

AWACS Airborne Warning And Control System. An aircraft based on a Boeing 707 airframe, carrying a powerful radar that can detect targets at ranges of up to 400 kilometres.

Ayatollah Senior cleric in *Shi'a* religion, not exclusive to Iran.

Ba'ath Pan-Arab socialist movement founded in Syria, 1944. Rival Ba'ath parties in power in Iraq and Syria.

Baseej Mass movement of Iranian youths, some only teenage, designed to supplement other Iranian armed forces. Several hundred thousand strong. Given minimal military training and only very light weapons.

Blitzkrieg Intensive military attack designed to defeat the opposition quickly.

Exocet French-made anti-ship missile. Used extensively by Iraq in attacks on Iranian shipping in the Gulf.

Gulf Co-Operation Council Founded 25 May 1981. Consists of Saudi Arabia, Kuwait, Oman, the UAE, Qatar, and Bahrain. Originally intended primarily as an economic grouping, but has become more defence orientated during Gulf War.

Human waves Mass formations of lightly-armed Iranians, intended to compensate for Iran's relative lack of equipment, and designed to overwhelm Iraqi defences by sheer weight of numbers.

Islam The Muslim religion; also refers to all the countries where the Muslim religion is dominant.

Kurds Separate ethnic and linguistic group inhabiting mountainous region in north-eastern Iraq, north-western Iran, and borders of Syria, Turkey, and the Soviet Union. About 15-20 million strong, want independent Kurdistan.

Pasdaran Iranian Revolutionary militia, bore brunt of initial Iraqi invasion. Look set eventually to replace regular armed forces on land, sea, and in the air.

Reflagging Re-registration of a ship's ownership with a company in another country, making it eligible to fly that country's flag and receive protection from its navy.

Sanctions Penalty imposed on a country, usually by blockading all dealings with it in a particular field—finance, trade, culture or military aid.

Scud-B NATO codename for a Soviet-designed ground-to-ground missile employed by Iran to attack Baghdad and other Iraqi cities.

Shi'a Muslims who pay allegiance to the prophet Muhammad's son-in-law, Ali. They represent a majority in Iran and Iraq, but are in a considerable minority in the Muslim world as a whole.

Silkworm A Chinese-made anti-ship missile, developed from an old Soviet design. Has a particularly powerful warhead. Iran stationed Silkworms, which are fired from mobile launchers on land, in the Strait of Hormuz and at the head of the Gulf. China repeatedly denied American charges that it supplied the weapons.

Sovereignty A legal concept meaning that the person or state possessing it has the right to do as it likes with the territory it controls.

Sunni Regarded as the 'orthodox' Muslims. By far the majority in the Muslim world. Follow the *Sunna*, or 'the way of the prophet'.

Thalweg Has no single definition in international law, but generally regarded as the 'median line' or main 'mid channel' of a river.

War of attrition Prolonged conflict in the hope of wearing down the enemy to achieve victory.

War of the cities Campaign of Iraqi air raids on Iranian cities, notably Tehran, to which Iranians have generally replied with missile attacks on Baghdad. Chief outbreaks in early 1984, first half of 1985, late 1986, early 1987 and 1988.

Further Reading

Chubin, Shahram and Tripp, Charles, *Iran and Iraq: War, Society, and Politics 1980–86* (PSIS Occasional Papers No 1/86).

Chubin, Shahram et al, *Security in the Gulf* (Gower, 1982).

Cordesman, Anthony H., *The Gulf and the Search for Strategic Stability* (Westview, 1984).

Cordesman, Anthony H., *The Iran–Iraq War and Western Security 1984–87* (RUSI/Jane's, 1987).

El Azhary, M. S. (Ed), *The Iran–Iraq War* (Croom Helm, 1984).

Hiro, Dilip, *Iran Under the Ayatollahs* (Routledge & Kegan Paul, 1985).

Joffe, George and McLachlan, Keith, *Iran and Iraq: The Next Five Years* (The Economist Publications, 1987).

Karsh, Efraim, *The Iran–Iraq War: A Military Analysis* (IISS, 1987).

Mansfield, Peter, *The Arabs* (Penguin, 1985).

Marr, Phebe, *The Modern History of Iraq* (Westview/ Longman, 1985).

McLachlan, Keith and Joffe, George, *The Gulf War* (The Economist Publications, 1984).

Nonneman, Gerd, *Iraq, The Gulf States, & the War* (Ithaca, 1986).

Petersen, J. E., *Defending Arabia* (Croom Helm, 1986).

Pridham, B. R. (Ed), *The Arab Gulf and the West* (Croom Helm, 1985).

Schofield, Richard N., *Evolution of the Shatt al-Arab Boundary Dispute* (Menas, 1986).

The Middle East and North Africa 1988 (Europa Yearbooks, 1987).

Index

Picture Acknowledgements

The publishers would like to thank the following for the loan of their photographs in this book: Associated Press 52; Camera Press 12–13, 23, 43, 50; Gamma 42; the *Guardian* 58; Christine Osborne 47; Popperfoto frontispiece, 8–9, 11, 15, 26–27, 29, 31, 53, 56, 60, 63, 68; The Research House 59; Topham 16–17, 19, 22, 25, 28, 32, 33, 34–5, 36–7, 38, 40, 44–5, 48, 54, 57, 64–5, 67, 69, 70–1. The maps on pages 10, 18, 20, 41 and 62 are by Malcolm S. Walker.